Indian fast food

ISBN: 978-81-7436-497-5

© This edition Roli & Janssen BV 2011
Second impression
Published in India by Roli Books in arrangement
with Roli & Janssen BV
M-75, Greater Kailash II Market
New Delhi - 110048, India
Phone: ++91-11-40682000
Fax: ++91-11-29217185
Email: info@rolibooks.com
Website: www.rolibooks.com

Editor: Neeta Datta
Design: Nitisha Mehta
Layout: Nabanita Das
Production: Naresh Nigam & Kumar Raman

Printed and bound in China

Indian fast food

Text: Pushpesh Pant
Photographs: Dheeraj Paul

Lustre Press
Roli Books

For my beloved granddaughter, Sara, who is always in a hurry,

and a 'Fast Food Fan' from birth!

 # Contents

Introduction

Fast foods in India are very different from what this genre means in the West. Of course, the recipes are quick to cook but that is where the similarity ends. Be it hamburgers, hot dogs or fish 'n' chips, even pizzas, most of the popular items are seldom prepared at home. These are quintessential 'street fare' more often than 'assembled' from pre-cooked or at least semi-processed ingredients. For decades these have become standardized for the mass-market proprietary products. All that is required is to turn the patty or grill the sausage. Such fast food fills the belly and can even contribute to some fun and frolic when shared with family and friends. And while it is easy to become addicted to this fare rare would be the person who finds real satisfaction.

Indian fast foods, in contrast, are not to be grabbed on the run and swallowed mindlessly. Time saving Indian recipes should not be confused with, or confined to, snacks and street-side eats. They are an integral part of everyday cooking at home. They require little time to prepare and cook; the emphasis is on starting from scratch and relying on seasonally appropriate fresh ingredients. Indian culinary repertoire takes pride in a unique palate of tastes comprising six basic flavours (*shadras*) – sweet, sour, bitter, salty, pungent, and astringent. What is amazing is that even when pressed for time no compromise is made in this regard. Care is taken to let the diner revel in sublime stimulation provided by these various palate stimulants and mood manipulators.

No one can accuse Indian fast foods of being junk food. There is no dearth of recipes in various regional culinary repertoires that serve as nourishing one-dish meals that are easily prepared without much hassle. These recipes are firmly based on the dietary wisdom of Ayurveda – ancient Indian science and art of life – and can be enjoyed all the year round in harmony with changing cycle of seasons and according to the 'mood at the moment'. The most interesting thing about these recipes is that these can be very easily adapted as per individual requirements and do not depend on any indispensable, exotic ingredient. A substitute can often be pressed into service while cooking abroad without any appreciable difference in its impact.

We should not lose sight of the fact that most recipes for Indian fast foods are not a one-dish meal – though some suit this purpose. A quick cooking dish is paired with *roti*, *puri* or *paratha* in the wheat-loving North and in the realm of rice extending along the eastern seaboard and Southern India these are paired with it. This does not mean that the preparation of the meal is delayed. In most houses dough is kept ready or the small quantity needed to feed 2-3 persons can easily be kneaded in 5-7 minutes as the accompaniment is cooking. Similarly, rice is boiled if that is preferred. Traditionally, home made pickles and chutneys along with a bowl of yoghurt or raita and sliced onions, green chillies are served with the meal.

What is fascinating about Indian fast foods is that these have continued to evolve with passage of time. Many of the most popular items showcase fusion at its best. This blending of ingredients, cooking techniques is encountered regularly in these delicacies. The no-frills plain *paratha* is transformed into an exceptional offering when it holds within its caressing layers a filling fashioned with sweet green peas, cottage cheese, cauliflower or egg. The realm of Indian fast foods allows us to appreciate the vibrant cultural diversity of the subcontinent as well as the synthesizing genius of the people who dwell here.

Indian fast foods offer much more than convenient finger foods or a quick bite to quell the pangs of hunger. They cater, almost effortlessly, to different tastes and combine nutrition with ecstatic aesthetic experience. These recipes provide an opportunity to us all to improvise and innovate exposing ourselves to an exciting variety that is the spice of life. Usually savoured informally, these delicious gems are akin to notes of music (*swar*) that are radiant themselves and can also be combined to create a melody of great beauty.

Vegetarian

Grilled Cottage Cheese Rectangles

Paneer Tash Kebab

Preparation time: 15 minutes ∽ Cooking time: 10-15 minutes ∽ Serves: 4

Ingredients:

Cottage cheese (*paneer*), cut into ¼"-thick pieces and shaped like playing cards
∽ **300 gm / 11 oz**

Yoghurt (*dahi*), hung
∽ **3 tbsp / 45 gm / 1½ oz**

Cumin (*jeera*) powder, freshly ground
∽ **1 tsp / 3 gm**

Kashmiri red chilli powder
∽ **½ tsp / 1½ gm**

Tomatoes
∽ **250 gm / 9 oz**

Vegetable oil
∽ **1 tbsp / 15 ml**

Garlic (*lasan*) cloves, peeled, crushed
∽ **2-3**

Green chillies, chopped
∽ **3-4**

Salt to taste

Clove (*laung*), mace (*javitri*) and cardamom (*elaichi*) powder (sprinklers)
∽ **½ tsp / 1½ gm**

Method:

1. Blend cumin and red chilli powders with the yoghurt by whisking with a fork. Then gently massage the cottage chesse pieces with this mixture. Keep aside for about 15 minutes.

2. Scald the tomatoes in boiling water, remove skin and pulp.

3. Heat the oil in a frying pan; add the garlic and green chillies. Add the tomato and cook to a sauce-like consistency with a pinch of sugar (if preferred) over low-medium heat till the raw smell of tomatoes disappear. Add salt to taste, stir.

4. Line a non-stick frying pan with a thin film of oil and pan grill the cottage cheese till they begin to develop brown patches. Turn gently with a wooden spatula ensuring that they don't break.

5. Place the kebabs on a platter and top with tomato sauce. Drizzle with sprinklers.

Pickled Cottage Cheese

Thanda Achari Paneer

Preparation time: 15 minutes ∾ Cooking time: 15 minutes ∾ Serves: 4

Ingredients:

Cottage cheese (*paneer*), cut into 2" chunks
∾ **500 gm / 1.1 lb**

Yoghurt (*dahi*), whisked
∾ **2 cups / 500 gm / 1.1 lb**

Coriander (*dhaniya*) powder
∾ **1 tsp / 3 gm**

Turmeric (*haldi*) powder
∾ **a pinch**

Yellow or Kashmiri red chilli powder
∾ **1 tsp / 3 gm**

Salt to taste

Mustard (*sarson*) oil
∾ **3 tbsp / 45 ml / 1¹/₂ fl oz**

Mustard seeds (*rai*)
∾ **¹/₂ tsp / 1¹/₂ gm**

Onion seeds (*nigella*)
∾ **¹/₂ tsp / 1¹/₂ gm**

Fennel (*moti saunf*) seeds
∾ **1 tsp / 2¹/₂ gm**

Dried red chillies (*sookhi lal mirch*), cleaned with moist cloth and wiped dry
∾ **2**

Dried mango powder (*amchur*)
∾ **¹/₂ tsp / 1¹/₂ gm**

Green chillies, deseeded, slit
∾ **3-4**

Method:

1. Whisk the yoghurt in a bowl with coriander powder, turmeric powder, red chilli powder, and salt. Keep aside.

2. Heat 2 tbsp mustard oil in a pan; add the mustard, onion and fennel seeds. When the seeds begin to splutter, add dried red chillies, and stir-fry until the chillies change colour.

3. Now add the cottage cheese and dried mango powder; stir-fry until the moisture evaporates. Remove from heat, stir-in the yoghurt mixture.

4. Pour the remaining mustard oil on top and serve garnished with green chillies.

Cottage Cheese Cooked with Green Gram

Paneer ki Bhurji

Preparation time: 15 minutes ∾ Cooking time: 10 minutes ∾ Serves: 4

Ingredients:

Fresh green gram (*cholia*), boil until al dente
∾ **300 gm / 11 oz**

Cottage cheese (*paneer*), mashed
∾ **450 gm / 1 lb**

Ghee
∾ **¼ cup / 50 gm / 1¾ oz**

Cumin (*jeera*) seeds
∾ **1 tsp / 2 gm**

Onions, chopped
∾ **90 gm / 3 oz**

Ginger (*adrak*) paste, strained
∾ **2½ tsp / 15 gm**

Garlic (*lasan*) paste, strained
∾ **2½ tsp / 15 gm**

Kashmiri red chilli powder
∾ **1 tsp / 3 gm**

Turmeric (*haldi*) powder
∾ **½ tsp / 1½ gm**

Tomatoes, chopped
∾ **1 cup / 175 gm / 6 oz**

Green chillies, seeded, cut into ⅛" thick strips
∾ **4**

Salt to taste

Black peppercorns (*sabut kali mirch*), coarsely grounded
∾ **1 tsp / 4 gm**

Green cardamom (*choti elaichi*) powder
∾ **a generous pinch**

Clove (*laung*) powder
∾ **a generous pinch**

Nutmeg (*jaiphal*) powder
∾ **a generous pinch**

Dried fenugreek leaves (*kasoori methi*) powder
∾ **a generous pinch**

Ginger, cut into juliennes
∾ **15 gm / 1½" piece**

Green coriander (*hara dhaniya*), finely chopped
∾ **¼ cup / 12½ gm**

Method:

1. Heat the ghee in a wok (*kadhai*); add cumin seeds and stir on medium heat until these begin to pop. Add onions, sauté until light golden.

2. Add the ginger and garlic pastes, stir-fry until the moisture evaporates. Add red chilli powder and turmeric powder (dissolved in 2 tbsp water), and stir-fry until the moisture evaporates.

3. Add tomatoes, stir-fry until the moisture evaporates. Add fresh green gram and sauté until the fat leaves the sides. Now add cottage cheese, green chillies, and salt; stir-fry for a minute.

4. Add all the spice powders and stir. Remove and adjust the seasoning.

5. Transfer to a flat dish and serve hot garnished with ginger and green coriander and accompanied with roti.

Cottage Cheese Cooked in a Wok

Kadhai Paneer

Preparation time: 25 minutes ∾ Cooking time: 7-8 minutes ∾ Serves: 4

Ingredients:

Cottage cheese (*paneer*), cut into 2" x ¹/₂" x ¹/₂" batons
∾ **800 gm / 28 oz**

Ghee
∾ **3 tbsp / 45 gm / 1¹/₂ oz**

Onions, chopped
∾ **90 gm / 3 oz**

Garlic (*lasan*) paste, strained
∾ **3¹/₂ tsp / 20 gm**

Ginger (*adrak*) paste, strained
∾ **1³/₄ tsp / 10 gm**

Coriander (*dhaniya*) seeds, roasted, pounded to split
∾ **1 tsp / 2 gm**

Black peppercorns (*sabut kali mirch*), freshly roasted, coarsely grounded
∾ **1 tsp / 4 gm**

Kashmiri red chilli powder
∾ **1 tsp / 3 gm**

Turmeric (*haldi*) powder
∾ **¹/₂ tsp / 1¹/₂ gm**

Tomato purée, canned
∾ **1¹/₂ cups / 360 gm / 12 oz**

Green pepper (*Shimla mirch*), cut into ¹/₈"-thick strips
∾ **1**

Yellow bell pepper, cut into ¹/₈"-thick strips
∾ **1**

Red bell peppers, cut into ¹/₈"-thick strips
∾ **1**

Salt to taste

Cumin (*jeera*) powder
∾ **³/₄ tsp / 2¹/₄ gm**

Green cardamom (*choti elaichi*) powder
∾ **¹/₂ tsp / 1¹/₂ gm**

Mace (*javitri*) powder
∾ **¹/₈ tsp**

Cinnamon (*dalchini*) powder
∾ **¹/₈ tsp**

Clove (*laung*) powder
∾ **¹/₈ tsp**

Dried fenugreek leaves (*kasoori methi*) / Fenugreek seeds (*methi dana*)
∾ **a generous pinch**

Green coriander (*hara dhaniya*), chopped
∾ **1 tbsp / 4 gm**

Method:

1. Heat the ghee in a wok (*kadhai*); add the onions and sauté until translucent and glossy. Add garlic and ginger pastes, and stir-fry until the moisture evaporates. Add coriander seeds and black pepper powder; stir-fry until the seeds begin to change colour. Add red chilli and turmeric powders dissolved in 2 tbsp water, and stir-fry until the moisture evaporates.

2. Add tomato purée and salt; stir-fry until specks of fat begin to appear on the surface. Add cottage cheese, stir for a minute. Add the bell peppers and stir for a minute. Sprinkle the cumin, cardamom, mace, cinnamon, clove and dried fenugreek leaf powders; stir carefully, remove and adjust the seasoning.

3. Transfer to a serving dish and serve garnished with green coriander and accompanied with tandoori roti or *chapatti*.

Potato Delight

Aloo ki Tarkari

Preparation time: 10 minutes ∾ Cooking time: 10-15 minutes ∾ Serves: 4

Ingredients:

Potatoes, boiled, mashed
∾ **500 gm / 1.1 lb**

Vegetable oil
∾ **¹/₂ cup / 120 ml / 4 fl oz**

Asafoetida (*hing*)
∾ **a small pinch**

Cloves (*laung*)
∾ **6**

Bay leaf (*tej patta*)
∾ **1**

Turmeric (*haldi*) powder
∾ **1 tsp / 3 gm**

Cumin (*jeera*) powder
∾ **1 tsp / 3 gm**

Kashmiri red chilli powder
∾ **1 tsp / 3 gm**

Dried mango powder (*amchur*)
∾ **¹/₂ tsp / 1¹/₂ gm**

Ginger (*adrak*), scraped,
crushed
∾ **2" piece**

Salt to taste

Dried fenugreek (*kasoori methi*)
leaves, soaked in water and
crumbled
∾ **3 tbsp / 4¹/₂ gm**

Green chillies, deseeded
∾ **a few**

Green coriander (*hara dhaniya*),
for garnishing

Method:

1. Heat the oil in a wok (*kadhai*); add asafoetida and cook till it dissolves. Add cloves and bay leaf; fry for 20 seconds.

2. Add the spice powders mixed with little water and ginger; fry for another 30 seconds. Add about 4 cups water and bring to the boil.

3. Add mashed potatoes and salt. Reduce heat and cook till desired consistency is obtained. Sprinkle dried fenugreek leaves and mix well.

4. Serve hot garnished with green chillies and green coriander.

Mashed Potato-Tomato Duet

Aloo Tamatar ka Chokha

Preparation time: 10 minutes ∾ Cooking time: 10-15 minutes ∾ Serves: 4

Ingredients:

Potatoes, boiled, peeled
∾ **250 gm / 9 oz**

Tomatoes, medium-sized
∾ **4-6**

Green chillies, finely chopped
∾ **4**

Ginger (*adrak*), finely chopped
∾ **1" piece**

Kashmiri red chilli powder
∾ **¼ tsp**

Salt to taste

Mustard (*sarson*) oil
∾ **1 tbsp / 15 ml**

Green coriander (*hara dhaniya*)
∾ **a large sprig**

Vegetable oil for tempering, optional

Cumin (*jeera*) seeds for tempering, optional
∾ **½ tsp / 1 gm**

Method:

1. Blend in the green chillies, ginger, red chilli powder, salt, and mustard oil with the potatoes. Use hands to mash really well.

2. Char grill the tomatoes on open flame, peel and discard skin; then mash.

3. Heap the mashed potato mixture on a plate, arrange the mashed tomato decoratively and garnish with green coriander. You can temper the mixture with cumin seeds, if desired.

Stuffed Potatoes

Bharwan Aloo

Preparation time: 15 minutes ∾ Cooking time: 10-15 minutes ∾ Serves: 4

Ingredients:

Potatoes, large, peeled
∾ **6**

Vegetable oil for deep-frying

Black cumin (*shah jeera*) seeds
∾ **¹/₂ tsp**

Cottage cheese (*paneer*),
crumbled
∾ **200 gm / 7 oz**

Salt to taste

Kashmiri red chilli powder
∾ **¹/₄ tsp**

Dried mint (*pudina*), crushed
∾ **a large pinch**

Garam masala, optional
∾ **¹/₄ tsp**

Raisins (*kishmish*), washed,
stems removed
∾ **1 tsp**

Pine nuts (*chilgoza*), shelled
∾ **1 tsp**

Red bell pepper or medium
tomato, washed, cored, cut into
small diamonds
∾ **¹/₄**

Method:

1. Scoop out the core of the potatoes ensuring that about 1 cm remains intact. Reserve the core for some other use.

2. Heat the oil in a thick-bottomed deep pan; fry the potato shells till they acquire a golden hue and appear crisp. Remove and drain the excess oil on absorbent kitchen towels.

3. Heat a little oil in a non-stick pan; add black cumin seeds and when these splutter add the cottage cheese and quickly stir-fry for about 2 minutes. Sprinkle salt, red chilli powder, and dried mint along with garam masala, if using. Add raisins, pine nuts, and tomato or bell pepper. Mix well to blend. Remove from heat and fill the hollowed potatoes with this mixture.

Mushrooms Cooked with Onions

Khumb Dopyaza

Preparation time: 10 minutes ✤ Cooking time: 10-15 minutes ✤ Serves: 4

Ingredients:

Button mushrooms, large
✤ **400 gm / 14 oz**

Butter
✤ **1 tbsp / 15 gm**

Dried red chillies (*sookhi lal mirch*), wiped clean with moist cloth
✤ **2-3**

Onions, medium-sized, finely sliced
✤ **2¹/₂ cups / 250 gm / 9 oz**

Salt to taste

Green chillies, deseeded, slit lengthwise
✤ **2**

Ginger (*adrak*), scraped, washed, cut into strips
✤ **2" piece**

Method:

1. Wash the mushrooms well to remove all grit then wipe dry. Trim the stalks but do not cut or slice.

2. Melt the butter in a pan and first glaze the dried red chillies in it, remove and reserve. Add the onions in the same butter when hot. Stir continuously till the onions are translucent. Now add the mushrooms and salt. Stir-fry over high heat for about 3 minutes or till the moisture evaporates. Then add the green chillies and dried red chillies.

3. Serve hot garnished with ginger. Resist the temptation to add any other spices / herbs. Mushrooms have a delicate flavour of their own that should not be smothered. If you like a little sauce-like gravy do not evaporate all the moisture while stir-frying the mushrooms. Whatever else you do avoid tomatoes – these mushrooms are not to be paired with toast!

Mushrooms Draped in Yoghurt Sauce

Khumb Shabnam

Preparation time: 10 minutes ∽ Cooking time: 20 minutes ∽ Serves: 4

Ingredients:

Button mushrooms
∽ **200 gm / 7 oz**

Yoghurt (*dahi*)
∽ **200 gm / 7 oz**

Kashmiri red chilli powder
∽ **1 tsp / 3 gm**

Cumin (*jeera*) powder
∽ **1 tsp / 3 gm**

Aromatic Kashmiri garam masala, optional
∽ **1 tsp / 3 gm**

Turmeric (*haldi*) powder
∽ **a pinch**

Salt to taste

Vegetable oil
∽ **1 tbsp / 15 ml**

Green chillies, slit lengthwise
∽ **2**

Method:

1. Wash the mushrooms well or wipe with wet cloth to remove grit, pat dry then slice or quarter according to your preference.

2. Beat the yoghurt with the powdered spices and keep aside.

3. Coat a non-stick frying pan with a thin film of oil and heat. Put the mushrooms in and stir-fry over high heat till only a little moisture remains. Take care that the mushrooms do not scorch or dry up. Remove from heat and allow the mushrooms to cool. Pour in the spiced beaten yoghurt and mix.

4. Serve hot garnished with slit green chillies and accompanied with rice or roti.

Mushrooms Cooked in Vegetable Stock

Khumb Qorma

Preparation time: 20 minutes ∾ Cooking time: 10 minutes ∾ Serves: 4

Ingredients:

Button mushrooms, washed
∾ **800 gm / 28 oz**

Yoghurt (*dahi*)
∾ **¹/₂ cup / 125 gm / 4 oz**

Kashmiri red chilli powder
∾ **1 tsp / 3 gm**

Coriander (*dhaniya*) powder
∾ **1 tsp / 3 gm**

Turmeric (*haldi*) powder
∾ **¹/₂ tsp / 1¹/₂ gm**

Ghee
∾ **5 tbsp / 75 gm / 2¹/₂ oz**

Garlic (*lasan*) paste
∾ **3¹/₂ tsp / 20 gm**

Ginger (*adrak*) paste
∾ **3¹/₂ tsp / 20 gm**

Fried onion paste
∾ **4 tbsp / 50 gm / 1³/₄ oz**

Cashew nut (*kaju*) paste
∾ **4 tsp / 20 gm**

Vegetable stock
∾ **4 cups / 1 lt / 32 fl oz**

Salt to taste

Method:

1. Whisk the yoghurt with the spice powders.

2. Heat the ghee in a pan; add the mushrooms and stir over medium heat for a minute. Add the garlic and ginger pastes, stir-fry until the moisture evaporates. Remove the pan from the heat, stir-in the yoghurt mixture, return pan to heat and stir-fry until the fat leaves the sides.

3. Add the fried onion paste, stir for a few seconds. Add cashew nut paste, stir-fry until the fat leaves the sides. Add the vegetable stock and bring to the boil. Lower heat and simmer, stirring occasionally, until reduced by a third.

4. Remove the mushrooms and pass the gravy through a fine mesh soup strainer into a separate pan. Return the gravy to heat, add the mushrooms and bring to the boil. Reduce heat to low, add salt and stir. Cook covered, stirring occasionally, until of coating consistency.

Stuffed Onions in Spicy Gravy

Kandhey ki Subzi

Preparation time: 20 minutes ∞ Cooking time: 15 minutes ∞ Serves: 4

Ingredients:

Onions, button, peeled, criss-cross incisions made on top for filling
∞ **1 kg / 2.2 lb**

Vegetable oil
∞ **3 tbsp / 45 ml / 1¹/₂ fl oz**

Cumin (*jeera*) seeds
∞ **1 tsp / 2 gm**

Garlic (*lasan*) paste
∞ **5 tsp / 30 gm / 1 oz**

Ginger (*adrak*) paste
∞ **2 tsp / 12 gm**

Green chillies, slit, deseeded, finely chopped
∞ **2**

Coriander (*dhaniya*) powder
∞ **1 tbsp / 9 gm**

Kashmiri red chilli powder
∞ **1 tsp / 3 gm**

Turmeric (*haldi*) powder
∞ **1 tsp / 3 gm**

Tomatoes, chopped
∞ **450 gm / 16 oz**

Dried fenugreek leaves (*kasoori methi*), crushed between the palms
∞ **a pinch**

For the filling: mix together
Dried mango powder (*amchur*)
∞ **1 tsp / 3 gm**

Turmeric powder
∞ **¹/₂ tsp / 1¹/₂ gm**

Coriander powder
∞ **1 tsp / 3 gm**

Salt to taste

Cumin powder
∞ **1 tsp / 3 gm**

Black rock salt (*kala namak*)
∞ **a pinch**

Kashmiri red chilli powder
∞ **¹/₂ tsp / 1¹/₂ gm**

Method:

1. Mix all the ingredients of the filling in a bowl. Pack equal quantities of the filling between the incisions of the onions and reserve for 10 minutes.

2. Heat the oil in a wok (*kadhai*); add the cumin seeds and stir over medium heat until these begin to crackle. Add the garlic and ginger pastes; stir-fry until the moisture evaporates. Add green chillies and stir-fry for a minute.

3. Add coriander, red chilli and turmeric powders (all dissolved in 3 tbsp water); stir for a minute. Add tomatoes and stir-fry until they are completely mashed.

4. Add the stuffed onions and salt, stir, reduce heat to low and cook covered, stirring occasionally, until the onions are cooked, but not squishy and soft. Sprinkle dried fenugreek leaves, stir, remove and adjust the seasoning.

Tangy Tomato Curry

Tamatar ka Qut

Preparation time: 10 minutes ∞ Cooking time: 20 minutes ∞ Serves: 6

Ingredients:

Tomatoes, chopped
∞ **1 kg / 2.2 lb**

Ginger (*adrak*) paste
∞ **1 tsp / 6 gm**

Garlic (*lasan*) paste
∞ **1 tsp / 6 gm**

Curry leaves (*kadhi patta*)
∞ **15-20**

Fenugreek seeds (*methi dana*)
∞ **¹/₂ tsp / 2¹/₄ gm**

Cumin (*jeera*) seeds, roasted,
grounded
∞ **1 tsp / 2 gm**

Vegetable oil
∞ **¹/₃ cup / 80 ml / 2³/₄ fl oz**

Onions, medium-sized, sliced
∞ **2-3**

Salt to taste

Turmeric (*haldi*) powder
∞ **1 tsp / 3 gm**

Kashmiri red chilli powder
∞ **1 tsp / 3 gm**

Sesame (*til*) seeds, roasted,
coarsely grounded
∞ **1 tbsp / 10 gm**

Gram flour (*besan*), lightly dry
roasted
∞ **2 tbsp / 20 gm**

For the tempering (*baghar*):
Dried red chillies
(*sookhi lal mirch*)
∞ **7-8**

Mustard seeds (*rai*)
∞ **¹/₄ tsp**

Cumin seeds
∞ **¹/₂ tbsp / 3 gm**

Fenugreek seeds
∞ **¹/₄ tbsp**

Onion seeds (*nigella*)
∞ **¹/₄ tbsp**

Curry leaves
∞ **8-10**

Method:

1. Boil 1 cup water in a pan. Add tomatoes, ¹/₂ tsp each of ginger and garlic paste, curry leaves, fenugreek seeds, and cumin powder; cook for 10 minutes. Pass through a strainer to obtain a fine purée.

2. Heat the oil in a pan; fry the onions till golden brown. Add the remaining ginger and garlic pastes and fry for about 2 minutes. Add the tomato purée, salt, turmeric powder, red chilli powder, and sesame seeds. Blend the roasted gram flour with a little water and stir it in. Add a little water, if required. The dish should have a thick soup-like consistency. Simmer for about 10 minutes over medium heat.

3. **For the tempering**, heat the oil; add all the ingredients. When the mustard seeds pop and the dried red chillies turn brown, add the tempering to the tomato preparation and cover.

4. Serve hot garnished with hard-boiled egg, if desired.

Corn Kernels with Mixed Greens

Makai Methi Makhani Palak

Preparation time: 20 minutes ∽ Cooking time: 10 minutes ∽ Serves: 4

Ingredients:

Baby corn (*makai*), cut into
1" pieces
∽ **32**

Fenugreek (*methi*), washed
well, chopped
∽ **450 gm / 16 oz**

Spinach (*palak*), washed,
chopped
∽ **450 gm / 16 oz**

Vegetable oil
∽ **4 tbsp / 60 ml / 2 fl oz**

Garlic (*lasan*) cloves, finely
chopped
∽ **6**

Ginger (*adrak*), finely chopped
∽ **1" piece**

Green chillies, deseeded, finely
chopped
∽ **4**

Cumin (*jeera*) seeds
∽ **1 tsp / 2 gm**

Fennel (*moti saunf*) seeds
∽ **1 tsp / 2¹/₂ gm**

Onions, chopped
∽ **1 cup / 100 gm / 3¹/₂ oz**

Coriander (*dhaniya*) powder
∽ **1¹/₂ tsp / 5 gm**

Lemon (*nimbu*) juice
∽ **1 tbsp / 15 ml**

Black peppercorns (*sabut kali
mirch*), freshly roasted, coarsely
grounded
∽ **¹/₂ tsp / 2 gm**

Nutmeg (*jaiphal*) powder
∽ **¹/₄ tsp**

Clove (*laung*) powder
∽ **¹/₂ tsp / 1¹/₂ gm**

Salt to taste

Method:

1. Heat the oil in a deep pan; add garlic, stir over medium heat until it begins to change colour. Add ginger and green chillies, stir for a few seconds. Add cumin and fennel seeds, stir for a few seconds and then add onions; sauté until onions are translucent.

2. Add baby corn and stir-fry for 2 minutes. Add coriander powder (dissolved in 1 tbsp water), stir until the moisture has almost evaporated. Add fenugreek and spinach; stir-fry until the moisture has almost evaporated. Now add lemon juice and powdered spices; stir well. Remove and adjust the seasoning.

Green Gram Fritters in Yoghurt Gravy

Moong Pakori ki Kadhi

Preparation time: 10 minutes ∽ Cooking time: 20 minutes ∽ Serves: 4

Ingredients:

Yoghurt (*dahi*), one-day old
∽ **200 gm / 7 oz**

Green gram (*moong dal*) flour
∽ **150 gm / 5 oz**

Salt to taste

Kashmiri red chilli powder
∽ **1 tsp / 3 gm**

Turmeric (*haldi*) powder
∽ **1 tsp / 3 gm**

Vegetable oil
∽ **4 tsp / 20 ml**

Cumin (*jeera*) seeds
∽ **1 tsp / 2 gm**

Asafoetida (*hing*)
∽ **a pinch**

Garlic (*lasan*) paste
∽ **2 tsp / 12 gm**

Green chillies, slit, deseeded
∽ **1 tsp**

Vegetable oil for deep-frying

For the tempering:
Ghee
∽ **1 tbsp / 15 gm**

Cumin seeds
∽ **1 tsp / 2 gm**

Dried red chillies
(*sookhi lal mirch*)
∽ **4**

Method:

1. Mix the yoghurt with 1 lt water. Add $1/3$ cup green gram flour, salt, red chilli and turmeric powders; blend well.

2. Heat the oil in a pan; add the cumin seeds, asafoetida, garlic paste, and green chillies. Stir for about 25 seconds over low heat. Add the yoghurt mixture and simmer until the mixture is cooked and is of pouring consistency.

3. Heat the oil for deep-frying. Make a medium-thick batter with the remaining green gram flour. Beat well, preferably with hands, and drop small ladlefuls in hot oil. Fry in batches till these fritters turn golden. Add to the yoghurt mixture and simmer for a few more minutes. Adjust the seasoning.

4. **For the tempering**, heat the ghee in a frying pan; add the cumin seeds. When the seeds start spluttering, then add dried red chillies. When the chillies change colour, pour the contents over the yoghurt mixture.

French Beans Flavoured with Coconut

Poriyal

Preparation time: 10 minutes ✎ Cooking time: 10-15 minutes ✎ Serves: 4

Ingredients:

French beans, fresh, soft
✎ **500 gm / 1.1 lb**

Vegetable oil
✎ **1 tbsp / 15 ml**

Salt to taste

Mustard seeds (*rai*)
✎ **1 tsp / 3 gm**

Tender coconut (*nariyal*), grated
✎ **2 tbsp / 20 gm**

Method:

1. Snip off the top and the tip of the beans and string them. Wash well and cut into small pieces.

2. Heat the oil in a shallow pan; add the mustard seeds. When these begin to splutter add the beans. Sprinkle salt, stir well and cook uncovered, stirring occasionally, till done. Sprinkle a few drops of water, if necessary.

3. Garnish with grated coconut before serving. If you prefer a mild sting, a few chopped green chillies may be added.

Pressed Rice with Vegetables

Poha Pulao

Preparation time: 10 minutes ∞ Cooking time: 10 minutes ∞ Serves: 4

Ingredients:

Pressed rice (*chiwda*), drenched
in water in a colander then
spread out delicately to dry
∞ **100 gm / 3¹/₂ oz**

Vegetable oil + for stir-frying
∞ **1 tbsp / 15 ml**

Mustard seeds (*rai*)
∞ **¹/₂ tsp / 1¹/₂ gm**

Turmeric (*haldi*) powder
∞ **¹/₄ tsp**

Kashmiri red chilli powder
∞ **¹/₂ tsp / 1¹/₂ gm**

Garam masala, optional
∞ **¹/₂ tsp / 1¹/₂ gm**

Cauliflower (*phool gobi*),
washed well, broken into
florets
∞ **150 gm / 5 oz**

Potato, medium-sized
∞ **1**

French beans, stringed, cut
∞ **100 gm / 3¹/₂ oz**

Carrots (*gajar*), medium-sized,
scraped, washed well, diced
∞ **2**

Green peas (*hara matar*),
shelled, lightly boiled
∞ **100 gm / 3¹/₂ oz**

Tomatoes, medium-sized,
quartered
∞ **2**

Cottage cheese (*paneer*),
optional
∞ **50 gm / 1³/₄ oz**

Sugar
∞ **1 tsp**

Salt to taste

Lemon (*nimbu*) juice
∞ **1 tbsp / 15 ml**

Green chillies, deseeded
∞ **2-3**

Green coriander (*hara dhaniya*)
∞ **a large sprig**

Ginger (*adrak*)
∞ **1" piece**

Method:

1. Heat the oil in a large, flat pan; add the mustard seeds and the powdered spices; mix well for 30 seconds. Add the pressed rice turning lightly with a flat spatula. Cover, reduce heat to very low and remove from heat in about a minute.

2. In another frying pan, heat some more oil and brown the cauliflower, then stir-fry the potatoes, French beans, carrots, and peas. Add the tomatoes and cook till the tomatoes are just scalded. Add the cottage cheese in the end, if using.

3. Stir in the sugar, salt, and lemon juice along with green chillies.

4. Arrange the mixture in layers in a serving dish alternating the pressed rice and vegetable mix.

5. Serve hot garnished with green coriander and ginger.

Vegetarian

Spicy Vegetables Served with Buttered Bread

Pav Bhaaji

Preparation time: 10 minutes ∞ Cooking time: 10-15 minutes ∞ Serves: 4

Ingredients:

Mini loaves (*pav*), sliced in the middle separated
∞ **6-8**

Butter
∞ **½ cup / 100 gm / 3½ oz**

Tomatoes, scalded in boiling water, skinned, mashed to pulp
∞ **500 gm / 1.1 lb**

Potatoes, boiled, mashed
∞ **250 gm / 9 oz**

Green peas (*hara matar*), boiled
∞ **100 gm / 3½ oz**

Cauliflower (*phool gobi*)
∞ **200 gm / 7 oz**

Kashmiri red chilli powder
∞ **1 tsp / 3 gm**

Garam masala
∞ **1 tsp / 3 gm**

Black rock salt (*kala namak*)
∞ **¼ tsp**

Coriander (*dhaniya*) powder
∞ **½ tsp / 1½ gm**

Cumin (*jeera*) powder
∞ **½ tsp / 1½ gm**

Salt to taste

Green chillies, deseeded, finely chopped
∞ **6**

Ginger (*adrak*), scraped, finely sliced
∞ **2" piece**

Green coriander (*hara dhaniya*), chopped for garnishing

Method:

1. Heat a thick, large griddle (*tawa*) and coat it with a thin film of butter by rotating the slab of butter all over. Place the sliced loaves on it and cook till slightly brown. Remove and flatten a little with a spatula.

2. Put about ¼ cup butter in the centre of the griddle, where it is the hottest. When really hot, add the tomato pulp, mashed potatoes and other vegetables. Add the spice powder and continue to mash with a spatula till extremely well blended. You may decide upon the consistency of the vegetables according to individual taste.

3. Serve hot garnished with green chillies, ginger and green coriander accompanied with the loaves and a small blob of butter, if desired.

Semolina Snack

Upama

Preparation time: 10 minutes ∽ Cooking time: 10 minutes ∽ Serves: 4

Ingredients:

Semolina (*suji*), coarse
∽ **1 cup / 200 gm / 7 oz**

Vegetable oil / Ghee
∽ **¹/₂ cup / 120 ml / 4 fl oz**

Ginger (*adrak*), grounded
∽ **1 tsp / 6 gm**

Green chillies, chopped
∽ **4**

Onions, finely sliced
∽ **2 cups / 200 gm / 7 oz**

Green coriander (*hara dhaniya*),
chopped
∽ **1 bunch**

Salt to taste

Juice of lemon (*nimbu*)
∽ **1**

For the seasoning:
Bengal gram (*chana dal*)
∽ **1 tsp**

Black gram (*urad dal*), husked
∽ **1 tsp**

Mustard seeds (*rai*)
∽ **¹/₂ tsp / 1¹/₂ gm**

Cumin (*jeera*) seeds
∽ **¹/₂ tsp / 1 gm**

Cashew nuts (*kaju*)
∽ **6-8**

Method:

1. Heat half the oil / ghee in a frying pan. Add ginger; stir. Add all the seasoning ingredients and sauté. Add green chillies and onions and cook over low heat for about 3-4 minutes.

2. Heat 2 cups water separately with salt in a bowl.

3. Add semolina to the frying pan. Pour the hot water over it, and stir continuously till all the water is absorbed. Add the remaining oil / ghee and green coriander; mix well and remove from heat.

4. Serve hot sprinkled with lemon juice.

Spicy Green Gram with Pressed Rice

Chunki Matar aur Chiwda

Preparation time: 30 minutes ∞ Cooking time: 3-4 minutes ∞ Serves: 4

Ingredients:

Green peas (*hara matar*)
∞ **800 gm / 28 oz**

Salt to taste

Sugar
∞ **a pinch**

Pressed rice (*chiwda*), cleaned, washed
∞ **150 gm / 5 oz**

Orange juice
∞ **4 tbsp / 60 ml / 2 fl oz**

Ghee / Butter
∞ **5 tbsp / 75 gm / 2¹/₂ oz**

Cumin (*jeera*) seeds
∞ **2 tsp / 4 gm**

Green chillies, slit, deseeded, finely chopped
∞ **2**

Ginger (*adrak*), finely chopped
∞ **4 tbsp / 30 gm / 1 oz**

Asafoetida (*hing*), reserved in 1 tbsp water
∞ **a generous pinch**

Dried mango powder (*amchur*)
∞ **2 tsp / 6 gm**

Sugar
∞ **1 tbsp / 15 gm**

Lemon (*nimbu*) juice
∞ **2 tbsp / 30 ml / 1 fl oz**

For the pressed rice masala: pounded to coarse powder
Cloves (*laung*)
∞ **4**

Cinnamon (*dalchini*), 1" sticks
∞ **4**

Black cardamom (*badi elaichi*)
∞ **5**

Method:

1. Boil the peas in enough water to cover; add salt and sugar. Cook the peas until al dente. Drain and refresh in iced water at the time of cooking.

2. Reserve the pressed rice in orange juice for 15 minutes.

3. Heat the ghee / butter in a wok (*kadhai*); add the cumin seeds and stir over medium heat until these begin to pop. Add green chillies, ginger, and asafoetida; stir for 30 seconds. Then add the green peas, stir-fry until the peas are devoid of moisture; sprinkle salt, dried mango powder, sugar, and the pressed rice masala; stir until incorporated.

4. Add the pressed rice along with orange juice and stir gently until mixed. Reduce heat to low and simmer, stirring occasionally and carefully for 1-2 minutes. Remove, adjust the seasoning, stir in the lemon juice before serving.

Non Vegetarian

Goan Fish Curry

Gomantak Curry

Preparation time: 1 hour ᢙ Cooking time: 30 minutes ᢙ Serves: 4

Ingredients:

Fish, cut into pieces
ᢙ **750 gm / 26 oz**

Lemon (*nimbu*) juice
ᢙ **1 tsp / 5 ml**

Turmeric (*haldi*) powder
ᢙ **1 tsp / 3 gm**

Salt to taste

Dried red chillies (*sookhi lal mirch*), soaked in 1 cup water for about 15 minutes
ᢙ **8**

Coconut (*nariyal*), grated
ᢙ **1 cup / 100 gm / 3¹/₂ oz**

Coriander (*dhaniya*) seeds
ᢙ **3 tsp / 6 gm**

Onions, 1 chopped and 1 finely sliced
ᢙ **2**

Cumin (*jeera*) seeds
ᢙ **1 tsp / 2 gm**

Garlic (*lasan*), chopped
ᢙ **1¹/₂ tsp**

Tamarind (*imli*) pulp
ᢙ **1¹/₂ tsp / 12 gm**

Vegetable oil
ᢙ **2 tbsp / 30 ml / 1 fl oz**

Tomato, puréed
ᢙ **1**

Green chillies, slit lengthwise
ᢙ **3**

Lady's finger (*bhindi*), optional
ᢙ **a few**

Method:

1. Mix the lemon juice with a pinch each of turmeric powder and salt. Rub this paste on the fish and marinate for about 30 minutes.

2. Grind the dried red chillies, coconut, coriander seeds, chopped onion, cumin seeds, remaining turmeric powder, garlic, and 1 tsp tamarind pulp extract to obtain a smooth paste. Use a little water in which the red chillies were soaked.

3. Heat the oil in a wide, shallow pan; stir-fry the sliced onion for 7-8 minutes. Add the spice paste and cook over moderate heat for 6-7 minutes, adding a little water if necessary, till the paste turns golden brown. Add 4 cups water and cook till the oil separates from the spices. Add tomato purée, green chillies, lady's finger (optional), and salt to taste; cook for about 6 minutes. Add the reserved tamarind water, if desired. Add the fish and cook until done.

4. Serve garnished with green coriander.

Fish Cooked in Mustard

Shorshe Maach

Preparation time: 20 minutes ∞ Cooking time: 15 minutes ∞ Serves: 6

Ingredients:

Fish (Rohu), cut into pieces, cleaned thoroughly
∞ **750 gm / 26 oz**

Salt to taste

Poppy seeds (*khus khus*)
∞ **1 tbsp / 9 gm**

Yellow mustard seeds (*rai*)
∞ **1¹/₂ tbsp / 14 gm**

Turmeric (*haldi*) powder
∞ **1 tsp / 3 gm**

Coconut (*nariyal*), fresh, diced
∞ **¹/₄**

Ginger (*adrak*)
∞ **³/₄" piece**

Garlic (*lasan*) cloves
∞ **6**

Green chillies, slit lengthwise
∞ **3-4**

Onion, coarsely chopped
∞ **1**

Coriander (*dhaniya*) powder
∞ **2 tsp / 6 gm**

Cumin (*jeera*) powder
∞ **2 tsp / 6 gm**

Kashmiri red chilli powder
∞ **1¹/₂ tsp / 4¹/₂ gm**

Vegetable oil
∞ **5 tbsp / 75 ml / 2¹/₂ fl oz**

Juice of lemon (*nimbu*)
∞ **¹/₂**

Salt to taste

Green coriander (*hara dhaniya*), chopped for garnishing
∞ **2 tbsp / 8 gm**

Method:

1. Sprinkle salt on the fish and keep aside for 20 minutes. Then rinse.

2. Toast the poppy seeds for 2 minutes on a griddle (*tawa*) over low heat. Then soak the seeds in little water for about 15 minutes and grind to obtain a fine paste.

3. Grind the poppy seed paste together with ¹/₂ cup water, mustard seeds, turmeric powder, coconut, ginger, garlic, green chillies, onion, coriander powder, cumin powder, red chilli powder, and salt.

4. Heat the oil over moderate heat and fry the spice paste for 6-7 minutes, stirring continuously and adding a little water, if required. Add 2 cups water and lemon juice. Simmer for 5 minutes over low heat. Adjust the seasoning. Add the fish and cook until done.

5. Serve hot garnished with green coriander.

Whole Stuffed Pomfret

Bhareli Saranga

Preparation time: 20 minutes ∞ Cooking time: 10 minutes ∞ Serves: 6-8

Ingredients:

Pomfret, whole, cleaned, washed, fins, head and tails removed
∞ **500 gm / 1.1 lb**

Dried red chillies (*sookhi lal mirch*), deseeded, soaked in 1 tbsp vinegar for about 15 minutes
∞ **4**

Cumin (*jeera*) seeds
∞ **1¹/₂ tsp / 3 gm**

Garlic (*lasan*) cloves
∞ **10-12**

Ginger (*adrak*)
∞ **1" piece**

Salt to taste

Sugar
∞ **1 tsp**

Vegetable oil
∞ **¹/₂ cup / 120 ml / 4 fl oz**

Method:

1. Make a marinade by grinding dried red chillies, cumin seeds, garlic cloves, ginger, salt, and sugar together. Rub the paste well inside the fish and keep aside for at least 20 minutes.

2. Heat the oil in a large frying pan; shallow-fry the fish over low heat for about 7 minutes on each side. Remove and drain the excess oil on absorbent kitchen towels.

3. Serve hot.

Fish in Onion Tomato Gravy

Macchi Kaliya

Preparation time: 20 minutes ∾ Cooking time: 30 minutes ∾ Serves: 4

Ingredients:

Fish, cut into 4 fillets
∾ **1 kg / 2.2 lb**

Vegetable oil
∾ **¹/₄ cup / 60 ml / 2 fl oz**

Onions, finely sliced
∾ **3**

Ginger (*adrak*), grated
∾ **3 tsp**

Garlic (*lasan*), crushed
∾ **4 tsp**

Salt to taste

Kashmiri red chilli powder
∾ **1¹/₂ tsp / 4¹/₂ gm**

Turmeric (*haldi*) powder
∾ **1¹/₂ tsp / 4¹/₂ gm**

Tomatoes, medium-sized, chopped
∾ **4**

Ground to a paste:
Coriander (*dhaniya*) seeds
∾ **3 tsp / 6 gm**

Dried red chillies
(*sookhi lal mirch*)
∾ **4-6**

Tamarind (*imli*), extract
∾ **1¹/₂ tbsp / 36 gm / 1¹/₄ oz**

Method:

1. Heat the oil in a pan; fry the onions till light brown. Add ginger, garlic, salt, red chilli and turmeric powders; continue to stir-fry for 2 more minutes. Add the spice paste, sprinkle a little water, cover and simmer for 3-4 minutes to blend the spices.

2. Add the tomatoes and fry till the liquid dries up somewhat and the tomatoes blend with the other spices. Add about 1 cup water. When the water comes to the boil, gently slide in the fish fillets. Reduce heat, cover and simmer for about 10 minutes, stirring occasionally and very gently, till the fish is cooked.

Fried Fish Amritsari Style

Amritsari Macchi

Preparation time: 1 hour ∾ Cooking time: 15 minutes ∾ Serves: 4

Ingredients:

Fish, preferably Sole, boneless
cut into medium-sized pieces
∾ **1 kg / 2.2 lb**

Gram flour (*besan*)
∾ **3 tbsp / 30 gm / 1 oz**

Garlic (*lasan*) paste
∾ **5 tsp / 30 gm / 1 oz**

Ginger (*adrak*) paste
∾ **3 tsp / 18 gm**

Kashmiri red chilli powder
∾ **1 tsp / 3 gm**

Carom (*ajwain*) seeds
∾ **3 tsp / 7¹/₂ gm**

Asafoetida (*hing*)
∾ **1 tsp**

Black peppercorns
(*sabut kali mirch*)
∾ **4 tbsp / 50 gm / 1³/₄ oz**

Cumin (*jeera*) seeds
∾ **4 tbsp / 25 gm**

Black rock salt (*kala namak*)
∾ **4 tbsp / 60 gm / 2 oz**

Dry mint (*pudina*) leaves
∾ **5 tsp**

Tartaric
∾ **³/₄ tsp**

Dried mango powder (*amchur*)
∾ **150 gm / 5 oz**

Ginger powder (*sonth*)
∾ **4 tsp / 12 gm**

Yellow chilli powder
∾ **1 tbsp / 9 gm**

Salt to taste

Vegetable oil for deep-frying

Method:

1. Mix gram flour, garlic paste, ginger paste, red chilli powder, 1 tsp carom seeds, ¹/₂ tsp asafoetida with about ¹/₄ cup water in a large bowl to make a thin batter. Apply evenly on the fillets and keep aside for about 30 minutes.

2. Mix the remaining ingredients (except oil) together and make a fine powder in a mortar and pestle. Transfer this into a clean bowl and mix well. Sieve and use 2 tbsp or more as per taste as a sprinkler just before serving and store remainder in a dry, airtight container.

3. Heat the oil in a pan; deep-fry the fish over medium heat until light golden. Remove and drain the excess oil on absorbent kitchen towels. When the pieces are cool, make one slit down the middle along the length and 4 slits across the breadth. Now, re-heat the oil and deep-fry the fish again until golden and crusty. Again remove all excess fat and oil and serve hot.

Grilled Chicken Breasts

Murgh ke Parchey

Preparation time: 30 minutes ∾ Cooking time: 10 minutes ∾ Serves: 4

Ingredients:

Chicken breasts, boneless
∾ **750 gm / 26 oz**

Ginger-garlic (*adrak-lasan*) paste
∾ **2 tbsp / 36 gm / 1¼ oz**

White pepper (*safed mirch*)
powder
∾ **1 tbsp / 9 gm**

Black cumin (*shah jeera*) seeds
∾ **1 tbsp / 7½ gm**

Vegetable oil
∾ **1 tbsp / 15 ml**

Yoghurt (*dahi*), hung
∾ **100 gm / 3½ oz**

Egg white
∾ **1**

Cream
∾ **200 ml / 7 fl oz**

Cardamom (*elaichi*) powder
∾ **½ tbsp / 4½ gm**

Mace (*javitri*) powder
∾ **¼ tbsp**

Green chillies, chopped
∾ **6-8**

Green coriander (*hara dhaniya*),
fresh, chopped
∾ **a large sprig**

Salt to taste

Butter for basting

Method:

1. Rub the chicken breasts well with the ginger-garlic paste mixed with half of the white pepper powder, black cumin seeds, salt, and oil. Keep aside for 15 minutes.

2. Blend the yoghurt, egg white, and cream to a smooth paste. Add salt, cardamom and mace powders, green chillies, green coriander, and the remaining white pepper powder. Marinate the chicken in this second marinade for 15 minutes.

3. Remove and pierce the chicken through a skewer and roast over a charcoal grill for 6-7 minutes.

4. Baste with melted butter and roast for another 3-4 minutes.

5. Serve hot with choice of salad and chutney.

Succulent Spicy Chicken Chunks

Choooza Boti Kebab

Preparation time: 30 minutes ∞ Cooking time: 10 minutes ∞ Serves: 4-6

Ingredients:

Chicken, boneless pieces cut
into small cubes
∞ **1 kg / 2.2 lb**

Raw papaya paste
∞ **1 tsp / 5 gm**

Salt to taste

Malt vinegar (*sirka*)
∞ **¼ cup**

Butter
∞ **2 tbsp / 30 gm / 1 oz**

For the marinade:
Yoghurt (*dahi*), hung, whisked
∞ **200 gm / 7 oz**

Ginger (*adrak*) paste
∞ **2 tbsp / 36 gm / 1¼ oz**

Garlic (*lasan*) paste
∞ **2 tbsp / 36 gm / 1¼ oz**

Red chilli paste
∞ **2 tbsp / 30 gm / 1 oz**

Garam masala
∞ **2 tsp / 6 gm**

Vegetable oil
∞ **¼ cup / 60 ml / 2 fl oz**

Salt to taste

Method:

1. Mix the papaya paste with salt and vinegar in a large bowl. Leave the chicken in this mixture for at least 15 minutes, ensuring that each chunk is well coated.

2. **For the marinade,** blend all the ingredients mentioned and marinate the chicken for another 15 minutes.

3. Heat the butter in a very shallow or wide, flat pan; add the chunks with the marinade and cook over low-medium heat, turning frequently with a spatula, for about 15 minutes or till very little moisture remains.

Shredded Chicken with Bell Peppers

Chooza Chaat

Preparation time: 15 minutes ❧ Assembly time: 5 minutes ❧ Serves: 2-3

Ingredients:

Chicken breasts, boneless, boiled or grilled cut into thin strips or shredded
❧ **200 gm / 7 oz**

Red bell pepper, medium-sized, washed, pat dry
❧ **1**

Yellow bell pepper, medium-sized, washed, pat dry
❧ **1**

Green pepper (*Shimla mirch*), medium-sized, washed, pat dry
❧ **1**

Garlic (*lasan*) cloves
❧ **3-4**

Lemon (*nimbu*) juice
❧ **1 tsp / 5 ml**

Olive oil
❧ **1/2 tsp**

Black peppercorns (*sabut kali mirch*), coarsely grounded
❧ **1/2 tsp / 2 gm**

Mustard paste (*kasundhi*)
❧ **1 tsp / 5 gm**

Low sodium salt
❧ **a small pinch**

Walnut (*akhrot*) kernels
❧ **1/4 cup / 30 gm / 1 oz**

Method:

1. Scald the peppers on open flame in the gas stove ensuring that these are charred evenly on all sides but not burnt to taste bitter. Place these in a plastic bag, seal tight and allow to 'weep' for about 10 minutes. Then remove from the bag, peel, halve and remove the pith. Cut into stripes or squares.

2. Place the chicken and the peppers in a bowl, sprinkle the other ingredients and toss well. Garnish with walnut kernels.

Spicy Liver

Kaleji Masala

Preparation time: 20 minutes ✎ Cooking time: 15 minutes ✎ Serves: 4

Ingredients:

Liver, sliced
✍ **500 gm / 1.1 lb**

Garlic (*lasan*) paste
✍ **2 tsp / 12 gm**

Ginger (*adrak*) paste
✍ **2 tsp / 12 gm**

Cinnamon (*dalchini*), 2" stick
✍ **1**

Green chillies
✍ **4-5**

Black peppercorns
(*sabut kali mirch*)
✍ **8-10**

Cumin (*jeera*) seeds
✍ **1 tsp / 2 gm**

Malt vinegar (*sirka*)
✍ **100 ml / 3¹/₂ fl oz**

Sugar
✍ **¹/₂ tsp**

Salt to taste

Ghee
✍ **¹/₂ cup / 100 gm / 3¹/₂ oz**

Onions, finely sliced
✍ **1³/₄ cups / 175 gm / 5³/₄ oz**

Tomatoes, large, finely chopped
✍ **2**

Method:

1. Put the liver in some water, add garlic paste, ginger paste, and cinnamon stick. Boil for about 10 minutes. Remove the pieces from the stock, wash and keep aside. Collect the residual stock for later use.

2. Prepare the marinade by mixing all the remaining ingredients except the last three. Apply this mixture on the liver pieces and keep aside for about 10 minutes.

3. Heat the ghee in a pan; add the onions, and sauté until golden brown. Add salt, liver with the marinade, and the stock. Bring to the boil. Add the tomatoes and cook till the water dries up.

Mashed Meat

Gosht ki Khurchan

Preparation time: 15 minutes ∽ Cooking time: 20 minutes ∽ Serves: 4

Ingredients:

Pasanda, boneless fillets from leg
∽ **500 gm / 1.1 lb**

Yoghurt (*dahi*), hung
∽ **2 tbsp / 30 gm / 1 oz**

Garlic-ginger (*lasan-adrak*) paste
∽ **1 tbsp / 18 gm**

Cumin (*jeera*) powder
∽ **1 tsp / 3 gm**

Kashmiri red chilli powder
∽ **1 tsp / 3 gm**

Garam masala
∽ **1 tsp / 3 gm**

Vegetable oil
∽ **3 tbsp / 45 ml / 1¹/₂ fl oz**

Onion, medium-sized, finely sliced
∽ **1**

Green chillies, finely chopped
∽ **2**

Ginger, scraped, finely diced
∽ **1" piece**

Dried red chilli (*sookhi lal mirch*), shredded, optional
∽ **1**

Salt to taste

Method:

1. Wash and pat dry the meat. Then with a sharp, heavy knife or small meat cleaver cut the *pasanda* into thin strips.

2. Blend the yoghurt, ginger-garlic paste with the powdered spices and marinate the *pasanda* strips in this mixture.

3. Heat the oil in a thick-bottomed frying pan and when it reaches smoking point lower heat and add the onions. When these begin to brown, add the meat with the marinade. Increase heat and stir-fry briskly for about 5 minutes. Use a large ladle to mash the meat at regular intervals as it cooks. Sprinkle green chillies and ginger along with the dried red chillies, if using. Lower heat and cook covered for another 5 minutes. Sprinkle a little water, if required. Remove when done to taste. Adjust the seasoning.

4. Serve accompanied with hot *chapatti* or *paratha* or on toast.

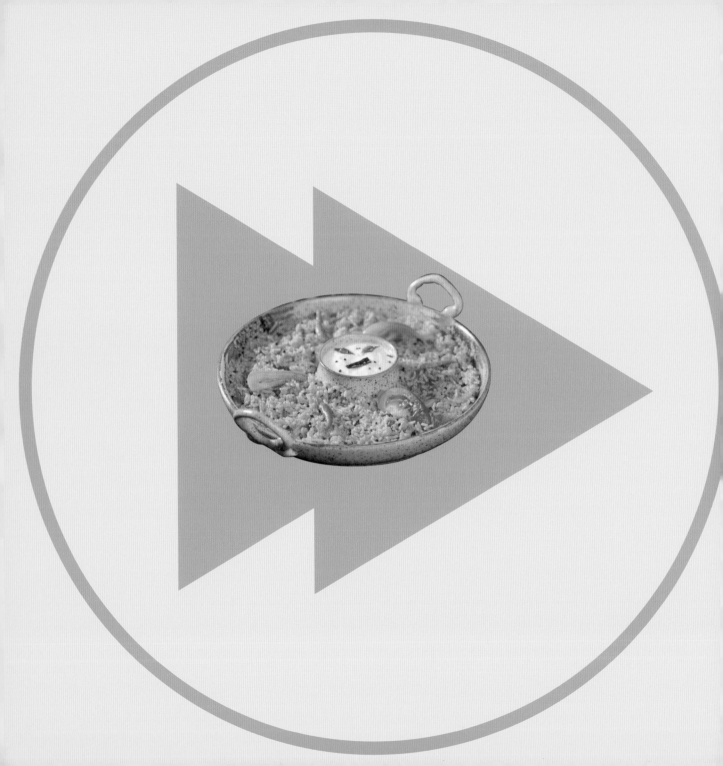

Rice and Breads

Tomato Rice

Tamatar Chawal

Preparation time: 15 minutes ✎ Cooking time: 15 minutes ✎ Serves: 4

Ingredients:

Rice, washed, soaked for 10 minutes
✎ **2¹/₂ cups / 500 gm / 1.1 lb**

Tomatoes, washed, quartered
✎ **200 gm / 7 oz**

Vegetable oil
✎ **3 tbsp / 45 ml / 1¹/₂ fl oz**

Mustard seeds (*rai*)
✎ **1 tsp / 3 gm**

Curry leaves (*kadhi patta*)
✎ **10-12**

Bengal gram (*chana dal*)
✎ **2 tsp**

Green chillies, chopped
✎ **4-6**

Turmeric (*haldi*) powder
✎ **¹/₂ tsp / 1¹/₂ gm**

Asafoetida (*hing*)
✎ **a pinch**

Kashmiri red chilli powder
✎ **1 tsp / 3 gm**

Salt to taste

Coconut (*nariyal*), freshly grated
✎ **5 tbsp / 50 gm / 1³/₄ oz**

Green coriander (*hara dhaniya*), chopped
✎ **a large sprig**

Method:

1. Boil the rice in salted water.

2. Heat the oil in a pan; add mustard seeds, curry leaves, Bengal gram, and green chillies; stir-fry over medium heat until the Bengal gram becomes light brown.

3. Add the tomatoes, turmeric powder, asafoetida, red chilli powder, and salt; stir for 15 seconds. Pour this mixture over the rice. Mix well.

4. Serve garnished with coconut and green coriander.

Pepper Flavoured Porridge

Pongal

Preparation time: 10 minutes ∽ Cooking time: 20 minutes ∽ Serve: 4-6

Ingredients:

Green gram (*moong dal*), dry roasted
∽ **1 cup / 200 gm / 7 oz**

Rice, coarsely grounded resembling semolina, dry roasted
∽ **2 cups / 400 gm / 14 oz**

Salt to taste

Vegetable oil / Ghee
∽ **¼ cup / 60 ml / 2 fl oz**

Asafoetida (*hing*)
∽ **a pinch**

Mustard seeds (*rai*)
∽ **1 tsp / 3 gm**

Dried red chillies (*sookhi lal mirch*)
∽ **3**

Curry leaves (*kadhi patta*)
∽ **8-10**

Cashew nuts (*kaju*)
∽ **10-15**

Black peppercorns (*sabut kali mirch*)
∽ **1 tsp / 3 gm**

Juice of lemon, optional
∽ **1**

Method:

1. Boil the green gram, drain and mash. Add ground rice, salt, and 4 cups water. Cook over low heat till the water is fully absorbed.

2. Heat the oil / ghee in a frying pan; add the asafoetida, dried red chillies, and curry leaves; sauté. Add cashew nuts and black peppercorns and fry for about a minute. Remove from heat and mix with the green gram mixture.

3. Transfer the mixture into a bowl and serve hot sprinkled with lemon juice, if desired.

Sago Flavoured with Coconut and Green Coriander

Saboo Dana Khichdi

Preparation time: 10 minutes ∾ Cooking time: 10 minutes ∾ Serves: 6

Ingredients:

Sago (*saboo dana*), washed, drained
∾ **2 cups / 400 gm / 14 oz**

Peanuts (*moongphalli*), roasted, crushed
∾ **2 cups / 280 gm / 10 oz**

Coconut (*nariyal*), fresh, grated
∾ **2 tbsp / 20 gm**

Cumin (*jeera*) seeds
∾ **1 tsp / 2 gm**

Sugar
∾ **¹/₂ tsp**

Black rock salt (*kala namak*)
to taste

Lemon (*nimbu*) juice
∾ **2 tsp / 10 ml**

Ghee / Vegetable oil
∾ **1¹/₂ tbsp / 25 gm**

Potatoes, finely chopped
∾ **2**

Green chillies, finely chopped
∾ **4-5**

Green coriander (*hara dhaniya*), chopped
∾ **3 tbsp / 12 gm**

Method:

1. Separate the sago for any lumps and sprinkle 1 cup water to loosen the sago and, if required, break the crumbs.

2. In a bowl, add peanuts, coconut, cumin seeds, sugar, rock salt, and lemon juice. Mix well and keep aside.

3. Heat the ghee / oil in a separate pan; stir-fry the potatoes till they become tender. Add the peanut mixture and cook for a few minutes. Add green chillies and continue to stir-fry for a while. Mix in the sago and cook covered for 5 minutes over very low heat with intermittent stirring. Remove from heat the moment the sago turns soft and transparent. Add green coriander and mix well.

4. Serve hot.

Every Day Vegetable Pulao

Subzion ki Taharee

Preparation time: 15 minutes ➣ Cooking time: 20 minutes ➣ Serves: 4

Ingredients:

Basmati rice
➣ **1¹/₂ cups / 300 gm / 11 oz**

Potatoes, medium-sized, peeled, washed, cut into quarters
➣ **6**

Cauliflower (*phool gobi*), cut into small pieces, blanched in boiling water, refreshed
➣ **100 gm / 3¹/₂ oz**

Carrots (*gajar*), cut into small pieces, blanched in boiling water, refreshed
➣ **100 gm / 3¹/₂ oz**

Green peas (*hara matar*), shelled, blanched
➣ **50 gm / 1³/₄ oz**

Ghee
➣ **5 tbsp / 75 gm / 2¹/₂ oz**

Green cardamom (*choti elaichi*)
➣ **4**

Cloves (*laung*)
➣ **3-4**

Cinnamon (*dalchini*), 1" stick
➣ **1**

Ginger (*adrak*) paste
➣ **5 tsp / 30 gm / 1 oz**

Garlic (*lasan*) paste
➣ **2¹/₂ tsp / 15 gm**

Fried onions
➣ **100 gm / 3¹/₂ oz**

Kashmiri red chilli powder
➣ **1 tsp / 3 gm**

Turmeric (*haldi*) powder
➣ **¹/₂ tsp / 1¹/₂ gm**

Tomatoes, large, chopped
➣ **3**

Green coriander (*hara dhaniya*), chopped
➣ **2 tbsp / 8 gm**

Mint (*pudina*), chopped
➣ **1 tbsp / 4 gm**

Green chillies, chopped
➣ **4**

Salt to taste

Lemon (*nimbu*) juice
➣ **1 tbsp / 15 ml**

For the muslin bag (*potli*):
Black peppercorns (*sabut kali mirch*)
➣ **12**

Fennel (*moti saunf*) seeds
➣ **2 tsp / 5 gm**

Green cardamom
➣ **5**

Black cardamom (*badi elaichi*)
➣ **4**

Cloves
➣ **4**

Bay leaves (*tej patta*)
➣ **2**

Cinnamon, 1" sticks
➣ **2**

Rice

Method:

1. Pick rice, wash in running water, drain, and reserve.

2. Boil the potatoes in enough water to cover with a pinch of turmeric powder, green chillies, and salt to taste until half cooked. Drain and pat dry.

3. **For the muslin bag (*potli*),** put all the ingredients in a mortar and pound with the pestle to break the spices. Fold in a piece of muslin and secure with enough string for it to hang over the rim of the pot.

4. Heat the ghee in a pan; add green cardamom, cloves, and cinnamon stick; stir over medium heat until cardamom changes colour. Reduce heat, add the ginger and garlic pastes, and stir until the moisture evaporates. Then add the blanched vegetables, stir. Add fried onions, and stir-fry for a couple of minutes. Add the red chilli and turmeric powders (dissolved in 2 tbsp water), stir, add water and bring to the boil. Reduce heat to low, and add tomatoes, green coriander, mint, and green chillies; stir.

5. Add rice and hang the muslin bag. Bring the mixture to the boil, reduce heat to low, add salt and stir. Sprinkle lemon juice, stir, cover and simmer (without stirring) until the rice is cooked and the water is fully absorbed.

6. Remove, discard the muslin bag and adjust the seasoning.

Rice Cooked with Red Gram

Bisi Bele Huli Anna

Preparation time: 15 minutes ∽ Cooking time: 20 minutes ∽ Serves: 4

Ingredients:

Rice, soaked for 15 minutes
∽ **2 cups / 400 gm / 14 oz**

Red gram (*arhar dal*)
∽ **1 cup / 200 gm / 7 oz**

Coriander (*dhaniya*) seeds
∽ **2 tsp / 4 gm**

Fenugreek seeds (*methi dana*)
∽ **1/2 tsp / 2 1/4 gm**

Coconut (*nariyal*), grated
∽ **1/4**

Bengal gram (*chana dal*)
∽ **1 tbsp / 12 gm**

Tamarind (*imli*), lemon-sized,
soaked in 1/2 cup water
∽ **1**

Ghee
∽ **1/2 cup / 100 gm / 3 1/2 oz**

Tomatoes, chopped
∽ **250 gm / 9 oz**

Drumsticks (*saijjan ki phalli*), cut
into 2" pieces
∽ **2**

Carrots, cut into 1/2" pieces
∽ **2**

Eggplants (*baingan*), cut into

1/2" pieces
∽ **4**

French beans, cut into 1/2" pieces
∽ **10**

Potatoes, cut into 1/2" pieces
∽ **4**

Green chillies
∽ **2**

Onions, small
∽ **250 gm / 9 oz**

Turmeric (*haldi*) powder
∽ **1/4 tsp**

Salt to taste

For the tempering:
Vegetable oil
∽ **1 tbsp / 15 ml**

Curry leaves (*kadhi patta*)
∽ **10**

Mustard seeds (*rai*)
∽ **1 tsp / 3 gm**

Asafoetida (*hing*)
∽ **a pinch**

Dried red chillies (*sookhi lal mirch*)
∽ **6**

Method:

1. Dry roast the coriander seeds, fenugreek seeds, coconut, and Bengal gram. Grind to a powder and keep aside. Squeeze out the tamarind pulp and strain.

2. Heat the ghee in a pan; fry all the vegetables, keeping the onions whole. Add the tamarind extract, the powdered spices, turmeric powder, and salt.

3. **For the tempering**, heat the oil in a pan; add the curry leaves, mustard seeds, asafoetida, and dried red chillies; sauté till dark brown. Remove and add to the vegetable mixture. Add rice and red gram and 8 1/2 cups water. Cook till the rice and gram are done. Remove and serve.

Rice Cooked with Minced Lamb

Keema Khichdi

Preparation time: 10 minutes ∞ Cooking time: 1 hour ∞ Serves: 4

Ingredients:

Lamb mince
∞ **250 gm / 9 oz**

Rice
∞ **1/2 cup / 100 gm / 3¹/₂ oz**

Ghee
∞ **4 tbsp / 60 gm / 2 oz**

Kashmiri red chilli powder
∞ **1 tsp / 3 gm**

Garlic (*lasan*) paste
∞ **1 tsp / 6 gm**

Ginger (*adrak*), grated
∞ **1/2" piece**

Yoghurt (*dahi*)
∞ **4 tbsp / 60 gm / 2 oz**

Onion paste
∞ **1 tbsp / 12 gm**

Black cumin (*shah jeera*) seeds
∞ **1/4 tsp**

Coriander (*dhaniya*) powder,
freshly crushed
∞ **1 tsp / 3 gm**

Cinnamon (*dalchini*),
cardamom (*elaichi*) and mace
(*javitri*) powders
∞ **a small pinch of each**

Onions, thinly sliced
∞ **30 gm / 1 oz**

Split green gram (*moong dal*),
husked / Red gram (*arhar dal*)
∞ **75 gm / 2¹/₂ oz**

Ginger, grated
∞ **1/2" piece**

Salt to taste

Method:

1. Heat 2 tbsp ghee in a thick-bottomed pan; fry the mince with red chilli powder, garlic paste, ginger, yoghurt, and onion paste till well browned. Add the spices with a little water. Put on *dum* and cook till the mince is tender and dry.

2. Heat the remaining ghee for the rice in a separate pan; fry the onions till golden, drain and keep aside. Fry the rice and green gram or red gram with ginger. Add water and salt, boil till half done. Put on *dum* and cook till almost done.

3. Spread the rice and green gram mixture over the mince, put the fried onions on top and cook on *dum* for another half hour. Sprinkle a little water or milk if necessary. Blend well before serving.

Slow Cooked Prawn Rice

Jhinga Biryani

Preparation time: 30 minutes ∽ Cooking time: 10-15 minutes ∽ Serves: 4

Ingredients:

Prawns (*jhinga*), shelled, deveined
∽ **250 gm / 9 oz**

Dried prawns
∽ **250 gm / 9 oz**

Salt to taste

Rice, drained, boiled in salted water till almost done
∽ **1 cup / 200 gm / 7 oz**

Vegetable oil
∽ **4 tbsp / 60 ml / 2 fl oz**

Onions, sliced
∽ **1¹/₂ cups / 150 gm / 5 oz**

Ginger (*adrak*), crushed
∽ **1" piece**

Garlic (*lasan*) cloves, crushed
∽ **10**

Green chillies, slit
∽ **10**

Sambhar masala
∽ **3 tbsp / 27 gm**

Coconut (*nariyal*) milk, thin
∽ **1 cup / 200 ml / 7 fl oz**

Tamarind (*imli*) extract
∽ **3 tbsp / 70 gm / 2¹/₄ oz**

Coconut milk, thick
∽ **¹/₂ cup / 100 ml / 3¹/₂ fl oz**

Method:

1. Mix the dried and fresh prawns with salt and keep aside for 30 minutes.

2. Heat the oil in a pan; add the onions, ginger, and garlic and sauté over low heat till golden brown, stirring continuously. Add the prawns and green chillies; stir-fry for 3-4 minutes.

3. Blend the *sambhar* masala with the thin coconut milk and add to the prawn mixture. Stir in the tamarind extract and mix well. Cook for about 10 minutes more. Remove prawns from the gravy and thicken the gravy by boiling it briskly. Stir in the thick coconut milk gradually.

4. Line a pan lightly with butter / oil. Put a layer of rice then the reserved prawns, top with rice and finish with prawns. Pour the thick gravy, cover and place on a preheated griddle for about 5 minutes.

5. Serve hot.

Fish Pilaf

Macchi Qorma Pulao

Preparation time: 15 minutes ✎ Cooking time: 20 minutes ✎ Serves: 4

Ingredients:

Fish (Surmai, Bhetki or
Singhara), boneless chunks
✎ **1 kg / 2.2 lb**

Rice, long-grained, washed,
drained, boiled till almost done
✎ **2¹/₂ cups / 500 gm / 1.1 lb**

Coconut (*nariyal*), desiccated
✎ **2 tbsp / 20 gm**

Poppy seeds (*khus khus*)
✎ **2 tbsp / 18 gm**

Mustard seeds (*rai*)
✎ **1 tsp / 3 gm**

Onions
✎ **1 cup / 100 gm / 3¹/₂ oz**

Green coriander (*hara dhaniya*),
fresh, chopped
✎ **¹/₂ cup / 30 gm / 1 oz**

Mint (*pudina*), fresh, chopped
✎ **1 cup / 30 gm / 1 oz**

Green chillies, chopped
✎ **4**

Ginger (*adrak*) paste
✎ **5 tsp / 30 gm / 1 oz**

Garlic (*lasan*) paste
✎ **3 tsp / 18 gm**

Yoghurt (*dahi*)
✎ **100 gm / 3¹/₂ oz**

Kashmiri red chilli powder
✎ **1 tsp / 3 gm**

Cumin (*jeera*) powder
✎ **1 tsp / 3 gm**

Salt to taste

Lemon (*nimbu*) juice
✎ **2 tbsp / 30 ml / 1 fl oz**

Ghee / Mustard oil if you prefer
✎ **¹/₂ cup / 120 gm / 4 oz**

Green cardamom (*choti elaichi*)
powder
✎ **¹/₈ tsp**

Clove (*laung*) powder
✎ **¹/₈ tsp**

Cinnamon (*dalchini*) powder
✎ **¹/₈ tsp**

Nutmeg (*jaiphal*) powder
✎ **¹/₈ tsp**

Black cumin (*shah jeera*)
powder
✎ **¹/₈ tsp**

Method:

1. Roast the coconut, poppy seeds, mustard seeds, and onions (with the skin), individually, until each emits its unique aroma and is lightly coloured. Put in a blender, add enough water and pulse into a moist but coarse paste.

2. Grind the green coriander, mint, and green chillies to a paste.

3. Put the two pastes in a bowl, add ginger paste, garlic paste, yoghurt, red chilli powder, cumin powder, salt, and lemon juice; mix well. Evenly rub the paste over the fish chunks and keep aside for 10 minutes.

4. Spread ghee / oil in a flat pan; put the fish along with the marinade. Add the spice powders; cover with a lid and cook on *dum* for 10-12 minutes or until cooked. Uncover and place the fish on top of the cooked rice, gently scooping out the rice to cover the fish pieces. Pour the gravy all over, cover and place on a hot griddle to finish for about 5 minutes. Serve hot.

Shallow Fried Bread Encased with Egg

Anda Paratha

Preparation time: 20 minutes ∽ Cooking time: 30 minutes ∽ Serves: 4

Ingredients:

Wholewheat flour (*atta*)
∽ **2 cups / 300 gm / 11 oz**

Ghee
∽ **1 tbsp / 15 gm**

Eggs, beaten
∽ **4**

Onions, small, chopped
∽ **2**

Green coriander (*hara dhaniya*), chopped
∽ **a sprig**

Salt to taste

Green chillies
∽ **2-3**

Vegetable oil for shallow-frying

Method:

1. Beat the eggs with onions, green coriander, salt, and green chillies. Keep aside.

2. Mix the wholewheat flour with 1 tbsp ghee and a little salt and knead with a little water to obtain a medium-soft dough.

3. Divide the dough equally into even-sized balls. Dust these balls with a little flour and roll out into discs of about 7" diameter. Brush lightly with ghee. Sprinkle over a little dry flour. Now fold ⅓ of the disc from one side and fold the other side over this. Sprinkle some more dry flour. Once again fold a portion from one side overlapping it with the other side to obtain a layered square. Dust it slightly again with flour and roll out into a 6" square bread.

4. Heat a little oil on a griddle (*tawa*); shallow-fry the *paratha* on both sides for about a minute. When the *paratha* is evenly fried and is rich golden in colour remove it to a plate and make a slit on one side with a sharp knife to create an envelope.

5. Spread some of the egg mixture inside and seal the opening by pressing on it. Place the *paratha* once again on the griddle and shallow-fry applying very little oil.

6. Repeat till all are fried

Spicy Peas and Cottage Cheese Stuffed Bread

Matar Paneer Paratha

Preparation time: 30 minutes ∞ Cooking time: 30 minutes ∞ Makes: 8-10

Ingredients:

Green peas (*hara matar*),
shelled, boiled, mashed
∞ **1 cup / 150 gm / 5 oz**

Cottage cheese (*paneer*),
crumbled
∞ **1 cup**

Ginger-chilli (*adrak-mirch*) paste
∞ **1 tbsp / 18 gm**

Green coriander (*hara dhaniya*),
chopped
∞ **1 tbsp / 4 gm**

Yoghurt (*dahi*), sour, hung
∞ **¹/₂ cup / 125 gm / 4 oz**

Asafoetida (*hing*)
∞ **a large pinch**

Sugar
∞ **1 tsp**

Kashmiri red chilli powder
∞ **¹/₂ tsp / 1¹/₂ gm**

Garam masala
∞ **1 tsp / 3 gm**

Salt to taste

Cream of wheat, roasted
∞ **500 gm / 1.1 lb**

Wheat flour to dust and roll

Ghee for frying
∞ **1 cup / 200 gm / 7 oz**

Method:

1. Mix the green peas with cottage cheese, ginger-chilli paste, green coriander, yoghurt, asafoetida, sugar, red chilli powder, garam masala, and salt. Keep aside.

2. Mix the flour with water and knead to obtain a semi-stiff dough. Divide the dough into walnut-sized balls and lightly roll these on the floured surface into discs of about 6" diameter.

3. Place equal portions of the green pea mixture in the centre of the discs and shape into small balls; roll again into discs.

4. Heat a little ghee on a griddle (*tawa*) and shallow-fry the *paratha* on both sides till golden brown. Serve hot.

Bread Enriched with Lentils

Missi Roti

Preparation time: 20 ∞ Cooking time: 5 minutes ∞ Serves: 4

Ingredients:

Bengal gram (*chana dal*),
cooked, mashed into paste
∞ **¹/₂ cup / 100 gm / 3¹/₂ oz**

Green gram (*moong dal*),
husked, cooked, mashed into
paste
∞ **¹/₂ cup / 100 gm / 3¹/₂ oz**

Wholewheat flour (*atta*)
∞ **3 tbsp / 30 gm / 1 oz**

Refined flour (*maida*)
∞ **2 tbsp / 20 gm**

Onion, finely chopped
∞ **5 tbsp**

Green chillies, finely chopped
∞ **3**

Ginger (*adrak*), finely chopped
∞ **1 tbsp / 7¹/₂ gm**

Green coriander (*hara dhaniya*),
fresh, chopped
∞ **3 tsp**

Turmeric (*haldi*) powder
∞ **¹/₂ tsp / 1¹/₂ gm**

Kashmiri red chilli powder
∞ **1 tsp / 3 gm**

Salt to taste

Ghee
∞ **3 tbsp / 45 gm / 1¹/₂ oz**

Method:

1. Mix the wheat flour and refined flour in a bowl. Add the dal pastes and the remaining ingredients expect ghee. Mix thoroughly, adding enough water, and knead into a soft pliable dough. Cover the dough with a light cloth and keep aside for about 10 minutes.

2. Divide the dough into 10 equal portions, shape into balls, dust with wholewheat flour, cover with a moist cloth and keep aside for another 5 minutes.

3. Flatten each ball between palms to a round disc, place on a cushioned pad (*gaddi*), stick inside a moderately hot tandoor and bake for about 4 minutes. Alternatively, you can place it in the pre-heated oven, on a greased baking tray and bake for about 6 minutes. Repeat till all are done.

4. Serve hot.

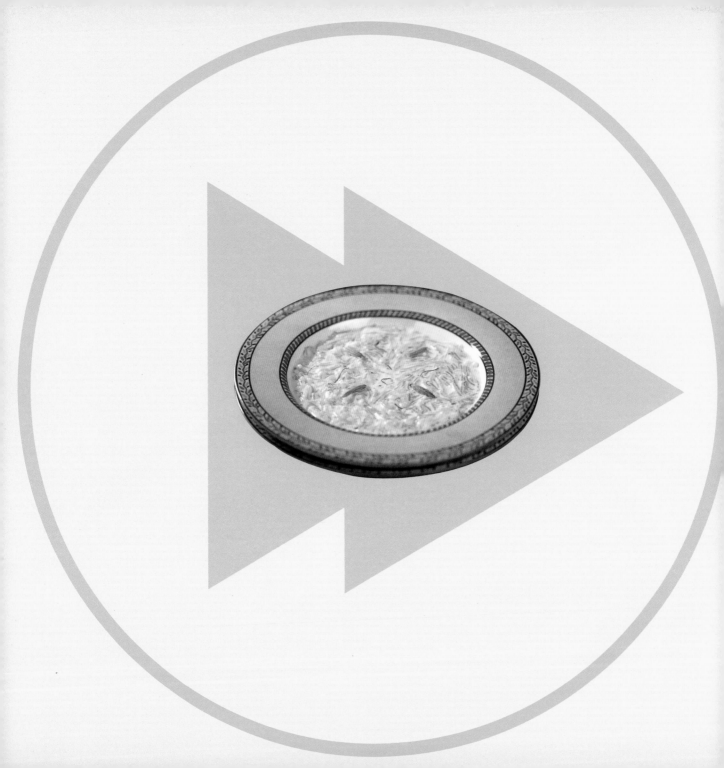

Accompaniments
and
Desserts

Tempered Yoghurt

Tarka Dahi

Preparation time: 10 minutes ∞ Cooking time: 10 minutes ∞ Serves: 4

Ingredients:

Yoghurt (*dahi*)
∞ **5 cups / 1¼ kg**

Vegetable oil
∞ **3 tbsp / 45 ml / 1½ fl oz**

Black mustard seeds (*rai*)
∞ **½ tsp / 1½ gm**

Coriander (*dhaniya*) seeds
∞ **½ tsp / 1 gm**

Dried red chillies
(*sookhi lal mirch*)
∞ **6-8**

Curry leaves (*kadhi patta*)
∞ **15-20**

Onions, finely chopped
∞ **3 tbsp**

Ginger (*adrak*), finely chopped
∞ **1" piece**

Green chillies, deseeded, finely
chopped
∞ **2**

Turmeric (*haldi*) powder
∞ **1 tsp / 3 gm**

Kashmiri red chilli powder
∞ **½ tsp / 1½ gm**

Tomatoes, finely chopped
∞ **75 gm / 2½ oz**

Salt to taste

Method:

1. Hang the yoghurt in muslin and once the whey is completely drained, transfer to a bowl, level with a spatula and keep aside.

2. Heat the oil in a wok (*kadhai*); add mustard seeds, coriander seeds, and dried red chillies, and stir over medium heat until the chillies become bright red. Add curry leaves and stir until they stop spluttering. Add onions and stir until translucent and glossy.

3. Add ginger and green chillies and stir until onions are lightly coloured. Then add turmeric and red chilli powders (dissolved in 2 tbsp water), and stir until the moisture evaporates. Now add tomatoes and salt and stir-fry until the moisture evaporates, remove and pour over the yoghurt cheese. Serve as an accompaniment.

Spinach Raita

Sabza

Preparation time: 15 minutes ∞ Cooking time: 10 minutes ∞ Serves: 4

Ingredients:

Yoghurt (*dahi*), neither sweet nor sour, whisked well
∞ **2 cups / 500 gm / 1.1 lb**

Spinach (*palak*), cleaned, washed well
∞ **500 gm / 1.1 lb**

Vegetable oil
∞ **1 tbsp / 15 ml**

Asafoetida (*hing*)
∞ **a pinch**

Mustard seeds (*rai*)
∞ **1 tsp / 3 gm**

Dried red chilli (*sookhi lal mirch*) for garnishing
∞ **1-2**

Black gram (*urad dal*), husked
∞ **2 tsp**

Green chillies, deseeded, finely chopped
∞ **2-3**

Curry leaves (*kadhi patta*)
∞ **a small sprig**

Method:

1. Boil the spinach with very little water in a pan. Remove, cool and discard stems.

2. Mix the spinach with the yoghurt and blend well with a wooden spatula, in a soup sieve.

3. Heat the oil in a pan; add the asafoetida and stir till it dissolves. Then add the mustard seeds, dried red chillies, black gram, green chillies, and curry leaves. When the seeds begin to crackle and the curry leaves and the chillies begin to change colour, pour this tempering over the yoghurt mix. Sprinkle salt according to taste. Remember that spinach has a salty taste and it is easy to over salt this dish.

4. Serve with rice or roti after the *sabza* has been chilled for a little while in the fridge. (You may increase the quantity of the dal used if you like more crunch.)

Green Leaves Enriched Yoghurt Curry

Bathua Kadhi

Preparation time: 20-30 minutes ✸ Cooking time: 20 minutes ✸ Serves: 4

Ingredients:

Bathua leaves, chopped
✎ **125 gm / 4 oz**

Yoghurt (*dahi*), one-day old
✎ **100 gm / 3¹/₂ oz**

Gram flour (*besan*)
✎ **2 tbsp / 20 gm**

Salt to taste

Kashmiri red chilli powder
✎ **1¹/₂ tsp / 5 gm**

Vegetable oil
✎ **4 tsp / 20 ml**

Cumin (*jeera*) seeds
✎ **1¹/₂ tsp / 3 gm**

Asafoetida (*hing*)
✎ **a pinch**

Garlic (*lasan*) paste
✎ **1³/₄ tsp / 10 gm**

Green chillies, slit, deseeded
✎ **3**

Turmeric (*haldi*) powder
✎ **1 tsp / 3 gm**

Method:

1. Dilute the yoghurt with approximately 1 lt water. Add gram flour, salt, and red chilli powder; turn and mix well.

2. Heat the oil in a pan; add the cumin seeds, asafoetida, garlic paste, green chillies and turmeric powder; sauté for 30 seconds over low heat.

3. Add the yoghurt mixture and *bathua* and simmer until the mixture is cooked and is of purée consistency. Adjust the seasoning.

Vermicelli Delight

Sevian

Preparation time: 10 minutes ❧ Cooking time: 10-15 minutes ❧ Serves: 4

Ingredients:

Vermicelli (*sevian*), fine variety, pre-roasted
❧ **500 gm / 1.1 lb**

Ghee / Unsalted butter
❧ **¹/₂ cup / 100 gm / 3¹/₂ oz**

Cloves (*laung*)
❧ **3-4**

Sugar
❧ **1 cup / 225 gm / 8 oz**

Water
❧ **2 cups / 500 ml / 16 fl oz**

Green cardamom (*choti elaichi*), seeds only, coarsely pounded
❧ **4-6**

Raisins (*kishmish*)
❧ **5 tbsp / 50 gm / 1³/₄ oz**

Saffron (*kesar*), soaked in ¹/₈ cup warm milk and crushed with the back of a spoon
❧ **a few strands**

Wholemilk fudge (*khoya*), grated
❧ **1 cup / 200 gm / 7 oz**

Almonds (*badam*), slivered
❧ **2 tbsp**

Pistachios (*pista*), slivered
❧ **2 tbsp**

Method:

1. Heat the ghee in a thick-bottomed pan; add the cloves. As the cloves change colour and swell, add sugar and water; bring to the boil. Reduce heat to medium low and add the green cardamom powder, raisins, and vermicelli broken into one-third their original size. Stir very gently and simmer till they soak in all the liquid.

2. Sprinkle the saffron with the milk. Remove the pan from the heat and very gently spread out the strands of vermicelli with a fork to ensure that these do not glue together in a gooey mess. Drizzle the wholemilk fudge evenly.

3. Serve garnished with almonds and pistachios.

Saffron Tinged Semolina

Kesari Bhaat

Preparation time: 10 minutes ✍ Cooking time: 10-15 minutes ✍ Serves: 4

Ingredients:

Granular semolina (*rava*)
✍ **2 cups / 400 gm / 14 oz**

Ghee
✍ **1 cup / 200 gm / 7 oz**

Cashew nuts (*kaju*)
✍ **10**

Sugar
✍ **2 cups / 450 gm / 1 lb**

Green cardamom (*choti elaichi*),
powdered
✍ **7-8**

Saffron (*kesar*), soaked in
¼ cup warm milk
✍ **a large pinch**

Method:

1. Heat the ghee in a pan; fry the semolina to a golden brown colour. Remove and keep aside. In the same pan, fry the cashew nuts.

2. Add 2-3 cups water (i.e. as much as necessary, depending on the quality of semolina used) to the fried semolina. Stir well and cook till most of the water is absorbed. Add sugar and cook till the mixture begins to stick to the spoon, leaving the sides of the vessel. Remove from heat.

3. Serve sprinkled with green cardamom powder, saffron mixture, and fried cashew nuts.

Sweet Rice Enriched with Dried Fruits

Zarda

Preparation time: 10 minutes ✑ Cooking time: 10-15 minutes ✑ Serves: 4

Ingredients:

Rice, long-grained, preferably
Basmati, soaked for 10 minutes
✑ **1 cup / 200 gm / 7 oz**

Sugar
✑ **100 gm / 3¹/₂ oz**

Water
✑ **¹/₂ cup / 125 ml / 4 fl oz**

Saffron (*kesar*), soaked in
lukewarm milk
✑ **a large pinch**

Raisins (*kishmish*), soaked in
water
✑ **1 tbsp / 10 gm**

Cashew nuts (*kaju*)
✑ **¹/₄ cup / 35 gm / 1¹/₄ oz**

Green cardamom (*choti elaichi*),
crushed after peeling
✑ **2-3**

Vetiver (*kewda*) essence / Rose
water (*gulab jal*)
✑ **a few drops**

Almonds (*badam*), peeled,
slivered
✑ **1 tsp**

Pistachios (*pista*), slivered
✑ **¹/₄ tsp**

Method:

1. Dissolve the sugar in water and cook to obtain a syrup ensuring that it does not become too thick.

2. Boil 1¹/₂ cups water in a pan. Add the rice and cook over medium heat, uncovered. When just about done, remove from heat, drain the water, taking care not to disturb the grains of rice.

3. Now stir in the syrup and crushed strands of saffron; gently turn the rice over with a wooden spatula. Sprinkle the raisins, cashew nuts, and crushed green cardamom. Cover and let it remain on very low flame, preferably over a pre-heated griddle (*tawa*) for about 10 minutes.

4. Sprinkle rose water or vetiver essence and serve garnished with almonds and pistachios. Enjoy hot or cold.

INDEX